Manifold V̄⎯⎯⎯⎯⎯⎯⎯.ŋoes

An Anthology

Compiled by
Eric Leslie

THE OAKWOOD PRESS

British Library Cataloguing in Publication Data
A Record for this book is available from the British Library
ISBN 0 85361 519 5

Typeset by Oakwood Graphics.
Repro by Ford Graphics, Ringwood, Hants.
Printed by Alpha Print (Oxford) Ltd, Witney, Oxon.

Weags Bridge & Grindon Station.

Published by
The Oakwood Press
P.O. Box 13, Usk, Mon. NP5 1YS

Contents

Introduction

Manifold Valley Railway, An Anthology is a collection of articles contributed by members of the erstwhile Manifold Valley Railway Society to a quarterly newsletter the 'Manifold Valley Echo'. Never intended to be anything more elaborate than a group of friends, with a common interest. The idea of forming the group grew out of the interest generated during the annual 'Steam in the Manifold' event.

Every summer, for three consecutive weekends, the sights and sounds of a steam locomotive working hard pulling its load of holidaymakers, daytrippers, even a fair sprinkling of railway enthusiasts, could once more be heard at Hulme End. This time it was on 10¼ in. gauge, but the attraction was just as strong. Eventually, almost a mile of portable track gave quite a good idea of what it must have been like to travel down the 'Secret Valley' by train. Smoke lingered in the overhanging trees and the whistle would set the echoes ringing back and forth around the limestone cliffs.

The other contributing factor was the impending threat to the last substantial bit of Manifold history still more or less in original condition - Hulme End station building site. Surplus to requirements, demolition and burning seemed to be its ultimate fate. Continued pressure by our group convinced the then owners of the whole site, Staffordshire Highways Authority, kindly to put in hand a first-aid package of repairs to halt the ravages of time, before a recent and very thorough restoration and re-paint in original colours.

The annual steam railway event was the result of tremendous effort, the bulk of which came from local employees of Belle Engineering at nearby Sheen. Their time was given voluntarily and the work of laying the track and moving heavy rolling stock went on after their normal working hours. Proceeds from all this - ticket sales etc. went to the Macmillan Fund.

Manifold Valley Railway, An Anthology is not technical - this aspect has been covered in other publications. This book is more an appreciation of the surrounding countryside, its people and their daily work, plus the huge number of visitors who take delight in what the area has in abundance - beautiful scenery and a sense of great peace.

Manifold Valley Railway, An Anthology will take the reader on a nostalgic trip along the route, through snippets of contemporary writing by friends and society members, many, sadly, no longer with us.

The events and people involved all pre-date 1934 so they were of an age group largely diminishing with the passage of time. How fortunate that their experiences are set down for us to savour in a world which they would nowadays barely recognise!

Manifold Valley Echoes are all around!

Many of the following contributions were given to me initially by word of mouth. I have tried to keep the format as close as possible to the original - with allowance for the difference between North Staffordshire and South Yorkshire dialect!

Eric Leslie
Barnstaple
Devon
1998

The Secret Valley

Eric Leslie

Most railway historians seem to be of the opinion that, apart from Hulme End station buildings, little is left of the Leek & Manifold Valley Light Railway. In terms of actual artefacts, this is so, but, to anyone with even the slightest powers of imagination, the railway lives on in its delightful location. The whole trackbed is still there, and, thanks to a far-sighted Sir Josiah Stamp of the LMS, open to walkers and, now, cyclists. Even the motorist is catered for by a short stretch between Butterton and Redhurst.

To cycle along the tarmac path today is to relive the journey more realistically than just walking, as one can feel, physically, the change of gradient. Free-wheeling from Hulme End is all very well until the return journey, which involves quite a sustained bout of pedalling.

But it is in the late summer evenings, when the crowds have gone, that the Manifold ghosts make their somewhat benign presence felt. The shadows lengthen, the high hills cast a cloak over the dry, hot stones of the river bed. Earlier in the day those same stones had gleamed white in the sun. Crowds picnicked on the grassy banks: now, however, all is quiet.

It seems the right thing to do is to tiptoe out and quietly close the door.

Where is the Manifold Valley?

Pages Magazine

The opening of the Leek & Manifold Valley Light Railway marks the introduction of a system of light railway construction which has been very successfully used in India, and also in the Barbados [*sic*], for the development of country which is too thinly inhabited to render an ordinary railway remunerative.

To the people of the Manifold Valley it means a great deal more, for they, not unnaturally, regard the railway as the harbinger of a new era of prosperity.

Before proceeding to describe the line and its formal opening by the Earl of Dartmouth last month, it will briefly consider the *locus in quo*.

Everybody has heard of Dovedale, but the Manifold Valley which, roughly speaking, may be said to be parallel with it, is to most people, a *terra incognita*.

Thanks to the light railway, thousands of excursionists will become acquainted with what is undoubtedly some of the finest scenery in North Staffordshire. The local farmers will be able to send in their produce at remunerative rates, and it is not altogether improbable that the copper mine at Ecton, one of the deepest in this country, may again add its quota of metal to the market.

The line traverses a district rich in minerals. It is to form a feeder line for the North Staffordshire Railway, but unfortunately, the branch of that railway between Leek and Waterhouses, with which it is to be connected, is not yet completed. In the meantime, a motor-car service has been established between those places.*

Waterhouses, the terminus of the light railway, is situated about midway between the town of Leek, which is upon the North Staffordshire Railway, and Ashbourne on the London & North Western Railway.

It will be obvious by a glance at the map of this district, that the ultimate objective of the railway must be Buxton, and it is understood that the Light Railway Company intend to apply for powers immediately to construct this extension. Mr Calthrop, the constructing engineer for the Light Railway Company, having already ridden over the ground, and mapped out the route which presents no great engineering difficulties, it is probable that more will be heard of the matter at an early date. The surrounding country presents all the features which make light railway enterprises desirable and place broad-gauge lines at a discount. For instance, from Leek to Buxton by road is about 12 miles; by rail it is something over 30.

The Earl of Dartmouth, speaking from the steps of a saloon, formally opened the line in the following terms: 'I declare the Leek & Manifold Valley Light Railway open for traffic with the most ardent hope that its success may exceed the wishes of the most sanguine supporters'.

---

* A Straker steam bus.

Building

Eric Leslie

Mr Forsyth, the original surveyor, seems to have been shabbily treated. From the records, it appears that he was never paid for the considerable amount of work he undertook. There is a letter from his son, complaining about his father's treatment and claiming expenses etc. Poor Forsyth senior died shortly afterwards.

The new man, Everard Richard Calthrop, came with an impeccable 'track record' and is said to have saved a considerable amoutn of money in actual construction. However, he still had to incorporate Swainsley Tunnel for no better reason than to hide the railway from the view of Sir Thomas Wardle of Swainsley Hall. Rather a close parallel to the demands of Sir George Newnes at Lynton and the siting of the Lynton & Barnstaple terminus out of sight of Hollerday House!

'I don't mind paying for the thing, but I definitely don't want to see it from my window!'

Or words to that effect.

Also, the choice of John Earle smacks of nepotism as Calthrop and Earle were brothers-in-law. John Earle was resident engineer to Calthrop's consultancy.

Again. Poor old Forsyth!

Opening

Eric Leslie

The line opened, after many difficulties, to great rejoicing and a banquet at Waterhouses.

Almost as a portent of what was to follow, the opening was reported, in great detail, in *The Times*. The only trouble was, it didn't actually take place! The whole thing was postponed until later.

Even then, only two coaches were available, the other two being unready for service and the open wagons rigged up with station seats were pressed into service.

The menus for the banquet have survived and provide an insight into such goings on. Particularly noticeable is the fact that the bigwigs dined for free whilst the poor ordinary people had to pay!

In his speech, the Duke of Devonshire, who was late arriving, extolled the virtues of the new line and assured everyone of its prosperity. He also urged the assembled guests to take up the shares on offer. I wonder if he took his own advice?

Sir Arthur Heywood, of minimum gauge fame, was one of the invited guests.

Tally-ho! for Buxton!

On to Buxton!

Eric Leslie

Perhaps if the goal of Buxton had been achieved things would have worked out better. Certainly, it would have been easier to explain to later generations just why the line terminated at such an isolated spot. Hulme End would have been halfway to Buxton and conveniently placed as a central depot.

Also, the land across the Hartington road belonged to the Harpur-Crewe family of Calke Abbey. Were they unwilling to let in an upstart North Staffordshire Railway branch, particularly as they appear to have been shareholders in the neighbouring London & North Western Railway (LNWR)?

For whatever reason, probably unwillingness on the part of the North Staffordshire Directors to authorise more expense, the line came to its ultimate finis at the hamlet of Hulme End, never to develop into a Stoke or Derby of a narrow gauge empire.

Be that as it may, plans were drawn up for a Buxton Extension. Calthrop even proposed gauntletting of Manifold track with the standard gauge LNWR route into Buxton!

The spectacle of the Manifold's tank engines pounding up through Longnor and along the shared track is one of the more exciting railway 'might have beens'.

A sharp peak towered above us ......

The 'Toy' Railway

North Staffordshire Railway Publicity Guide

The Leek & Manifold Valley Light Railway was opened for passenger traffic by Lord Dartmouth on Monday 27th June, 1904. Nine miles in length, and of 2 ft 6 in. gauge, with a minimum curve of four chains, and a maximum gradient of 1 in 40, it gives access to one of the loveliest and least known valleys in Staffordshire, while it forms a feeder line for the North Staffordshire Railway.

From Leek to Waterhouses a normal gauge railway has been constructed, the stations on which are Bradnop, Ipstones, and Waterhouses, the latter being the station for the Caldon Quarries. Between Leek and Waterhouses the scenery does not call for special mention. Professor Boyd Dawkins has identified the woolly rhinoceros, and the cave bear among the fossil bones discovered at Waterhouses recently.

The stations on the Light Railway are Waterhouses, Sparrowlee, Beeston Tor, Grindon, Thor's Cave, Wetton Mill, Butterton, Ecton (for Warslow) and Hulme End (for Hartington). At Hartington the London & North Western Railway Company have a station on their Buxton and Ashbourne branch line. The Light Railway, it should be mentioned, is worked by the North Staffordshire Railway Company.

Each train carries its own station master and ticket collector, and travels at the rate of 12 mph. The carriages are of two types, namely composite 1st, 3rd and guard's compartment, and 3rd class only. The composites are provided with seats for 22 third class passengers and eight first class. The third class have seating accommodation for 44 passengers.

In addition to this seating accommodation, both types are provided with outside, railed platforms, upon which passengers are afforded the pleasure of seeing the picturesque scenery through which this railway curves and climbs unfolded like a panorama before them.

The vehicles are electrically lighted, and fitted with automatic vacuum brakes. The locomotives are six-wheels coupled, having driving wheels 2 ft 6 in. in diameter, with a rigid wheelbase of only 6 ft. They have outside cylinders 11½ in. in diameter by 16 in. stroke, with a boiler pressure of 150 lb. per square inch. A two-wheel radial truck enables these engines to run round very sharp curves with safety and ease.

A novel feature on the light railway is the transportation car. This is for carrying standard gauge vehicles over the narrow gauge, thereby retaining all the advantages of the narrow gauge without the disadvantage and cost of trans-shipping goods.

This little but convenient light railway, by its startling, almost sensational, but absolutely safe insinuosities, reminds one of the zig-zags of the 'corkscrew' railway over the Semmering to Vienna, on which, according to a facetious engineer - the traveller can see the nape of his own neck, so continually winding is the line.

The ups and downs, and ins and outs, of the Leek & Manifold Railway yield, however, an exhilarating succession of fresh scenes that come upon the

Time for a chat - Ecton.

passenger as pictorial surprises. We have already enumerated the names of the stations between and Hulme End. Particularising them, we may cite Beeston Tor as a boldly featured example of limestone scarp. Thor's Cave is a wide cavity that occupies a commanding position on a well-nigh precipitous declivity, and from its portal we look down upon the meandering of the River Manifold, which, a little way further, disappears underground, leaving a dry, boulder-strewn bed and trout and grayling gasping in despair.

This capricious stream, after following a subterfluent course for several miles, breaks its rocky bondage and re-appears rejoicing in the grounds of Ilam Hall. Bubbling out of a deep limestone cleft, it joins the River Dove, from which it had been divorced until it can no longer preserve its freedom, and they become happily re-united.

There is an interesting allusion to this stream in Boswell's *Life of Dr Johnson* (1777).

> Dr Johnson obligingly proposed to carry me to see Ilam, a romantic scene, now belonging to a family of the name of Port, but formerly the seat of the Congreaves . . . I recollect a very fine amphitheatre, surrounded with hills covered with woods, and walks neatly formed along the side of a rocky steep, on the quarter next to the house, with recesses under projections of rock, overshadowed with trees: in one of which recesses, we are told, Congreave wrote his 'Old Bachelor'. We viewed a remarkable natural curiosity at Ilam; two rivers bursting near each other from the rock, not from immediate springs, but after having run for many miles underground.
>
> Plott, in his *History of Staffordshire*, gives an account of this curiosity; but Johnson would not believe it, though we had the attestation of the gardener, who said he had put in corks where the River Manifold sinks into the ground, and had caught them in a net, placed before one of the openings where the water bursts out.

Wetton is the next station. It gives easy access to the village of Alstonfield, near Mill Dale, where the exploration of Dove Dale begins. In the church is an ancient pew, erected by Charles Cotton; near the church the George Hotel adminsters to creature comforts.

Ecton (for Warslow) is the next stopping place. It is famous on account of its copper mine, which belongs to the Duke of Devonshire. The shafts on the steep hillside are a great depth, one sinking to 1,400 ft. In 1780 out of the profits of one year's produce from this mine, the fifth Duke of Devonshire built the Crescent at Buxton at a cost of £120,000. Close by is the Dale Mine. There is every probability of this mine being re-opened.

In the immediate neighbourhood there is an abundance of lime, coal and marble. Rich dairy farms also abound, and the miniature railway is sure to stimulate agricultural interests.

The terminus stations at Hulme End (where a hostel, 'The Light Railway Hotel') has been licensed gives access to Hartington, which is in touch with that idyllic dell, Beresford Dale. Hartington station is on the LNWR's line from Ashbourne to Buxton, with a most convenient train service.

Circular tours have been arranged in connection with the North-Western Railway from Buxton, and passengers may alight from and re-join the trains at any station *en route*, enabling them to visit the various places of interest in Dove Dale, all of which are a walking distance from the stations on the Manifold Valley Light Railway.

That the new district opened up by this 'Toy' railway will become immediately popular we have no doubt, as it excels in majestic grandeur its famous neighbour, the Dove.

Manchester City News

The Duke of Devonshire on Tuesday cut the first sod of a light railway which is to be constructed under the provisions of the Light Railways Act of the present Government in North Staffordshire.

The North Staffordshire Railway Company have projected a new line of full gauge, running from Leek brook to Waterhouses, and branching on the way to the Caldon Quarries. The light railway, which will be of 2 ft 6 in. gauge, will run from Waterhouses to Hulme End, near the Hartington station of the new Buxton line in Derbyshire, a distance of over nine miles, and will, it is hoped, develop a tourist as well as mineral and agricultural traffic. It is expected that the line will afterwards be connected with Buxton direct, via Monyash [!].

The Duke, in the course of a speech, said the average cost of railways in the UK was, he understood, about £50,000 per mile, and this light railway would be constructed for less than £4,000 a mile, while they would be satisfied if they earned £5 per mile per week.

[*The Manchester City News*, 7th October, 1899.]

Leek to Beresford Dale

Thorough Guide to the Peak District 1908

The North Staffordshire Railway Company having extended their line from Leek to Waterhouses (10 miles) and the Manifold Valley Light Railway being opened to Hulme End, the beautiful Manifold Valley is now made more accessible, and both the head of Dovedale and the Hartington district can be reached more readily from the west.

The light railway is eight miles long, and threads the valleys of the Hamps and the Manifold, the charming scenery of which can be enjoyed to the full as the carriages are nearly all window. There are stations at Waterhouses, Sparrowlee, Beeston Tor, Grindon, Thor's Cave, Wetton Mill, Butterton, Ecton and Hulme End.

This sequestered district has lost much of its quiet, pastoral charm through the crowds of trippers brought by the new line, but this, of course, was inevitable, and the pedestrian can now more easily reach the more secluded spots and find them still more frequented. There are refreshment rooms at Thor's Cave and Beeston Tor.

Near Beeston Tor, a limestone crag towering 200 ft above the river, the Hamps and Manifold unite when there is water enough: but in normal weather the Hamps disappears into 'swallets' in the same way as the Manifold conducts itself near Wetton Mill.

Throwley Old Hall (Earl Cathcart) near Beeston Tor, is of historical and architectural interest. Butterton (Temperance Hotel) and Ecton are near the Ecton copper mines, where gunpowder is said to have been used first for blasting: at present the mines are not worked.

From Hulme End station (hotel and café) it is two miles to Hartington.

Beresford Dale may be reached in two miles by an avenue turning right (south) out of the Hartington road, a short mile beyond Hulme End; or a bus (6*d*.) may be taken to Hartington, and the field path just below the village followed down the dale.

[Sent by Jack Bunce.]

'Toy Railway'

Eric Leslie

During the earlier part of this century, the term 'Toy Railway' was applied indiscriminately, to any railway other than standard gauge. Thus, important minor railways became labelled without any due regard to their usefulness or technical standing.

Today, the term has a patronising ring, but in the 1920s and 1903s it was quite acceptable, along with smoking during meals, Shirley Temple and Felix the Cat!

So the 'Toy Railway' trundled back and forth along its quiet valley - personifying, mouse-like, 'industry in quiet places'. Not-so-toy the location with its soaring limestone crags and 300 ft hills which, in places, rose sheer from the lineside itself.

Out of sight of roads and away from the main railway system, the 'Manifold' took on a relaxed attitude, as witness the stopping to pick mushrooms or chat to pretty girls haymaking.

However, the return to Waterhouses and the steep final climb out of the valley seemed to instil an air of importance. Exhausts became sharper, the plume of smoke and steam shot ever higher and the engine really started to raise the echoes as the Ashbourne road was crossed.

Right into the station, the pulling would have to be sustained before the brakes could be applied and the train brought to a stand. Across, on the standard gauge track, the branch train to Leek would be waiting: it, too, would have quite a climb to continue its journey.

'Toy Railway' or not, the handsome Manifold tank engines, in their red-brown livery, at the head of a train of primrose yellow carriages with richly coloured, leaded-light opening vents, gave their larger cousins a run for their money in the appearance stakes.

The Virgin Birth

Dr J.R. Hollick

Nowadays, it is hard to believe that such an event was taken quite seriously in the earlier years of this century, enough to warrant an inquiry by the religious establishment.

The circumstances are just as bizarre and consist of a local girl, her parents, the postman and, of all things, the Leek & Manifold Valley Light Railway.

The girl, finding herself to be pregnant, assured her parents that no-one else was involved and that what had happened was nothing short of a miracle! Her parents confided in the local vicar who took the matter further. Eventually a church inquiry was convened and, as a result, the family doctor was involved to keep matters on a worldly footing.

It appears the girl was sent to meet the train at Hulme End to pick up any post and send off any outgoing mail. At this time the train had a post box in the guard's compartment and the local postman also came to attend the mail.

This arrangement meant that for a short period, the girl and the postman were alone in the van. 'Just long enough!' were the findings of the doctor and the tribunal. The postman himself finally confessed all after questioning by the good doctor.

So, the miraculous properties of the railway were, indeed, 'Not proven'.

The Model Railway

Dr J.R. Hollick

Many railwaymen were amongst my patients and an excellent relationship was built up over the years. Sadly, railway work, by its very nature, was hazardous and many times, men suffered broken limbs.

Recovering from injuries like this was helped by patients being involved in the construction and operation of a model railway layout. Injured fingers constructing fiddly trackwork and painting scenery healed and were restored to full functioning much better. A life-long friend was a shunter from Uttoxeter who had lost all but one finger and thumb in an accident.

The medical origins of some of the model railway equipment made a good story on its own. Scenery is well represented and one particular scale 'hill' is known as 'Tom's nappy', which is what it was!

The model of Hulme End station has a good representation of the cast-iron urinal which once graced the platform end, even down to a male figure inside. He, poor soul, has been standing there for years, doing nothing.

'Nobby'

Dr J.R. Hollick

Ecton is one of those places where there is always an indefinable atmosphere. During the time of the light railway it also boasted a population of tramps. For some reason they seemed to congregate there and take up residence among the lanes and in the barns dotted around the fields.

Their numbers remained more or less constant over the years but a harsh winter could take its toll and I would often be called to some poor soul found by the roadside.

When the traffic census was undertaken for the light railway order, it makes one wonder if this itinerant population was, for this purpose, recorded as 'shedded at Ecton'. It would certainly have improved the figures for this otherwise sparsely inhabited valley.

'Nobby' was one of the regulars. I never knew his real name, nor did I ask. Every now and then he would be admitted overnight to hospital. There he would be cleaned up, given a meal and a night's rest. In the morning he would take himself off. I last saw him on the road to Uttoxeter, what became of him we'll probably never know.

Some Holiday!

Dr J.R. Hollick

When the LMS took over from the North Staffordshire Railway, the appearance of the railway changed with the new livery of maroon for the coaches and black for the locomotives.

The staff were also able to see some improvement in their lot with the introduction, for the first time in their working lives, of a week's holiday.

Having little money to start with, the men couldn't really make much of this new found time off so what did they do? The only thing they knew. They spent most of the week at the station watching the trains come and go and having a natter with their mates!

Wrong Way Round

Dr J.R. Hollick

On the occasion of *Calthrop's* visit to Crewe works for periodic heavy repair, the engine was returned to Waterhouses the wrong way round. Engines had always worked chimney-first to Waterhouses because of the fierce climb out of the valley. Fears of the firebox crown being uncovered as the water in the boiler surged towards the smokebox end were the reason behind this and, justifiably, the foreman at Hulme End urgently requested the engine be sent back for turning.

Crewe's reply was that Hulme End depôt had a perfectly good crane and that, to put it briefly, he should get on with it.

The foreman wasn't having that, so *Calthrop* returned to traffic as it was. With great trepidation the engine steamed bunker-first up the climb out of the Hamps valley.

To the great relief of all concerned, nothing happened and the engine thus ran for some years. *Calthrop*, for some reason, doesn't seem to have been used anywhere as much as *Earle* whichever way round it happened to be facing!

Family Feuds

Dr J.R. Hollick

The relationship between father and son, driver and guard respectively, is quite well known to have been, to say the least, strained.

When operations demanded some form of communication between these two, the poor old fireman was roped in as go-between. One day, however, it resulted in an accident.

A North Staffordshire railway van, a six-wheeler, was being unloaded off a transporter. The usual communication system prevailed. 'Tell our Frank to ease up a bit'

Back went the fireman, 'Your Frank says what for!'

'What's the ——— old fool up to.'

Tempers flared and the driver set off only to hear a loud crash and look back to see the loaded van half-on, half-off the transporter!

Now came the task of emptying the van before it could be got back onto the transporter. Full of milk churns, the job took ages, and then they all had to be put back in again. All this certainly did nothing to improve relations between father and son.

Bombs in Swainsley Tunnel

Eric Leslie

During World War II, Swainsley tunnel was taken over by the army, the railway having been taken up in 1937. It was used as an ammunition store, the portals at each end being plugged by a wall of sand bags. A sentry was on guard and the telephone connection could still be seen until recently.

I think the whitewashing of the tunnel stonework throughout dates from this time. The railway certainly wouldn't have bothered.

If the whole thing had gone up in smoke, Swainsley Hall would have been the first man-made object in space!

Carriage Lights

Colin Plant

One of the most noticeable things about the ride was the almost constant ringing noise, very faint, as we went along.

At first I thought I had something wrong with my ears until I looked up and saw the little ornamental glass shades on the lamps were slowly revolving with the motion of the carriage, causing the whole thing to vibrate gently and give off the sound.

"I found Hulme End Station as we turned a corner of the road two miles from the village of Hartington."

The Peak: Some Places and People

B. Casson & Jean Thorburn

I have found a railway. It is about 20 miles long and has 10 stations. It took me 1¼ hours to reach it by car from Sheffield, 50 minutes to go the full length of the line, half-an-hour's rest, and 50 minutes back. There was a day of adventure for you!

I found Hulme End station as we turned a corner of the road two miles from the village of Hartington. The railway rejoices in the name of the Leek & Manifold Valley Light Railway. This was on a brass plate on the engine, which, when I arrived, was puffing softly to let the engine driver know that all was well and ready for the start.

The engine driver, meanwhile, was sitting on the kerbstone, which marks the difference between the platform and the railroad, reading his morning paper. He was a cheery soul, with very blue eyes and white teeth and he enjoys his railway, I am quite sure of that.

It has existed since 1904, and he has spent nine years as a driver, so he knows a good deal about it. At one time, he told me, the railway was the 'Milky Way' of the district. Hundreds of gallons of milk were carried from its little stations to the main line.

Now, there is no great distribution of milk, but Manchester 'hikers' love the railway, and so do the holiday parties, who leave their charabancs at Hulme End and do the railway trip while the cars proceed by a longer road to Waterhouses, and there pick them up.

About 500 holiday makers, mostly from the Potteries, travel on this line on August Bank Holiday. There are three trains a day, one in the morning, the next at 1 pm, and the third at 4 pm. I booked for the lunch-time train, and had three companions - a lady, a gentleman, and a little boy.

There was an air of great peace over the station until about 12.50, when everyone seemed to get busy at once. The station master and a porter suddenly remembered about a load of coal and a couple of carriages which should be elsewhere, so the engine driver got busy and his mate began shunting these obstacles.

Now this railway is a small gauge affair, but the coal wagons are of the ordinary size, so they have to be brought on 'transports', which are iron platforms fitting the small gauge lines to take the wagons. There is one siding with ordinary gauge, and the wagons had to be landed there while the extra carriages had to be put in the shed, in case they were blistered by the sun. All this took 20 minutes and the guard didn't like it. He wanted to run to time.

At 1.20 we were off down the valley of the lost rivers. The coach was divided into first and third class. There was a slight difference in the upholstery, and as the engine ran backwards on this journey, the first class got more smoke which didn't really matter, as we were all third class passengers.

My companion, the photographer, deserted me for the front of the train, where he stood on a little platform to get some of the views. I watched the beauties of the Manifold Valley, softly rounded hills, with wooded slopes, a

"At one time --- the railway was the "Milky Way,"
of the district." Hundreds of gallons of milk were carried.

Manchester "Hikers" love the railway.....

"We passed a field where a snow-white tent shone
in the sun" - - - - -

river with crystal clear water, a profusion of wild flowers. We passed a field where a snow-white tent shone in the sun, and we rolled along in the heart of the valley.

The engine driver ignored the stations on the way out; we passed Ecton (for Warslow) almost before I noticed it. Several of the stations were not marked by buildings, merely by signs, and others are important enough to have sheds for shelter. Butterton was next, and then a tunnel. Then, Wetton Mill, where children with bouquets of forget-me-nots waved to us from a nearby field.

Somewhere near here I noticed that we no longer saw the river, only a dry watercourse which we crossed and re-crossed for the rest of the way. Dry, dusty stones looked hot in the sun, plantations spread their shade over the dry river, and here and there tufts of grass and dried moss were on the rounded stones, while the well-built stone bridges looked quite out of place and useless. We came to Redhurst Crossing. In front I saw hills grow higher and lose their roundness.

A sharp peak towered above us and we reached Thor's Cave, which was high up on the left. Then we came to Grindon, and then to Beeston Tor, then to Sparrowlee, and we were running out of the valley to see a wider sweep of the country.

We had to cross a main road and that took time, as the fireman got down and closed the gates against the traffic. After he had climbed back onto the engine we moved on a little, and the guard opened the gates and climbed back into the carriage. We moved on again, and in a minute or two drew up at Waterhouses, where the railway finds its big brother, the Leek railway. Here, too, we saw the river again. I asked the guard one or two questions about the stream, but he was not talkative and I was little the wiser.

"Then Wetton Mill, where children with bouquets of forget-me-nots waved to us from a nearby field." - - - - - - - - -

The engine driver and fireman exchanged greetings with a pretty girl who was making hay in the field.

But on our return to the train I met those cheery fellows who drive the engine, and they described the days when the water courses were full. They told me that had I walked a short distance from the village I should have seen the water of the Hamps suddenly disappear underground. Where it comes out no-one knows.

The Manifold does not present so great a mystery. It disappears near Wetton and comes out at Ilam, but the Hamps, after the pretty village of Waterhouses, disappears for good.

As we came back through the valley I pondered over this story. It is a fairy-tale in real life - the valley of the lost river, with its lovely woods and rich fields, its wild roses and forget-me-nots and meadow sweet. Its loveliness seems to smile at the mere humans who cannot know the secret of its river.

The flowers and the trees and the birds could tell of the watercourse, for in the quietness when no fussy little train with its freight of noisy human beings is about, they may hear the trickle of water underground.

I was awakened out of this dreamland by the train drawing up with a jerk. No one got off, no one got on, but the guard, the engine driver, and the fireman exchanged greetings with a pretty girl who was making hay in the field beside the railway. I do not wonder that they wanted to talk to her, she looked so cheery and brown and happy. Her rounded arms were a lovely brown against the lighter colour of her dress, and her wavy hair was unshaded by hat and unspoilt by 'perm'. We went on again but pulled up at Wetton, where the children with forget-me-nots climbed aboard.

They waved to the engine driver as he opened his little window and took coals from a tiny tender. Two men got on board, and as we had seven passengers instead of five, we were quite a company.

The guard came and took our tickets in silent sternness. How stupid we were to be excited or even interested in the valley he went through several times a day! The engine driver bade us a cheery 'Goodbye!' as we stepped out of the train, and hoped that we had enjoyed the run. The children waved their flowers at him and ran off laughing.

Rumour has it that this line is to be closed, but no one could tell us if this really was the case. The railway will go on: the engine puffs its way with its load of carriages and passengers, sometimes half a dozen, sometimes a hundred. But the Manifold Valley is lovely and mysterious, with its unknown railway and its lost rivers.

As we got into the car we took a look back at the green hills, with their fine trees, at the outline against the sky, and we turned to go towards the real world; for this ended our adventures on a day when we found a railway and lost two rivers.

[From a book of the same title published by J.W. Northend, Sheffield, 1933, submitted by Keith Turner.]

Ashbourne Road crossing.

Ashbourne Road Crossing

Doug Blackhurst

Nowadays it would be termed an operational hazard. Situated on a steeply-climbing, sharply-curved track, it crossed the main Waterhouses to Ashbourne Road which was, itself, a fairly steep hill just here.

Usually, engines of trains whistled well before making the final climb - to alert the porter at Waterhouses. Being quite some distance away, this individual had to jump on his bicycle and close the gates to road vehicles, to avoid the train having to stop and restart on the incline. He then re-opened the gates and whatever traffic was held up in those days could resume its journey.

With the timetable and the engine whistles to work to, things should have gone smoothly. In true Manifold fashion things didn't always work out like that. The porter's love-life frequently interfered with his crossing duties and many's the time he was to be seen breaking speed records in cycle-clips through Waterhouses as Harry Robinson leant on the whistle, anxiously watching out for the gates to open for him!

Clearing the Balconies

Dr J.R. Hollick

During school holidays and outings, trips along the line were organised. School parties would arrive by motor coach at Hulme End. After a ride on the train, they would be picked up at Waterhouses.

On fine days, the end balconies of the coaches were popular, the public being allowed to ride on them. Sometimes they were a source of trouble with the train crews. Those immediately behind the engine could torment the men on the footplate, throwing orange-peel and apple cores etc. Another target was the easily accessible brake wheels and the easy way they could be screwed down whilst on the move! When such activities got beyond a joke there was a sure-fire remedy.

'Wait till we get to Butterton' said the driver to his mate. Once there, a lump of oily cotton waste was thrown into the firebox, the door shut just as the regulator was opened and the train plunged into the darkness of Swainsley tunnel.

Emerging into the sunlight once more at the other end of the tunnel, there wasn't a sign of anyone - the coach balconies were completely empty and all the doors and windows firmly shut! From then on things quietened down and the rest of the trip passed peacefully.

The handbrakes were, however, a never-ending problem for the crews at such busy times.

[From Harry Robinson and Arthur Dowler.]

.. Outside, railed platforms, upon which passengers are afforded the pleasure of seeing the picturesque scenery.

Bradshaw Rules!

Jack Bunce

Timetables have always fascinated me ever since childhood, nearly 40 years involved with them behind the scenes of London buses didn't cure me and I can still study then purely for pleasure.

Recently, the Manifold line's 1904 opening timetable came under my scrutiny and I offer the follow observations.

Firstly, one wonders who compiled it, presumably the North Staffordshire Railway, whose steam buses were involved, lent its expertise to the Manifold Directors who were anxious to get the maximum potential out of their new line and rolling stock (and staff!). There is a complication in the Thursday and Saturday variations indicated by symbols and (very) small print. On other weekdays two morning round trips in quick succession with one more in late afternoon are given (making no provision for workers or schoolchildren). This service suffices for Wednesday (market day) allowing some 6 or 3½ hours in Leek where the bus served the market area more closely than the eventually-completed railway.

It is worth remembering that, in those days, passengers were more concerned with taking goods to market (see the market ticket luggage note) and the bus roof-rack would have been well filled.

On the Monday, Tuesday, Wednesday and Friday service each of the three trains in and out of Waterhouses is 'mirrored' by a steam bus journey (at a much slower speed) interchanging at the temporary terminus.

Saturday is a natural choice for additional and later journeys and presumably Thursday was also chosen because, as early closing day in Leek and the Potteries, there was a potential pleasure traffic of shop workers into the country.

There are additional afternoon and evening trains on those days making five in all but connecting with only four bus journeys - the otherwise 5.00 pm bus trip from Leek running at 2.15 pm and then having a three hour 'siesta' at Waterhouses (time perhaps for a photo-session in Ashbourne).

There is an extra bus journey in the evening of these days connecting with the extra evening train which reached Hulme End as late as 9.25 pm. Daylight then in summer but potentially in darkness at other times of the year - did they ever light the headlamps?

[This was to have been the first of a series of articles on the 'Manifold' timetables but, sadly, Jack Bunce died before he could complete any further articles.]

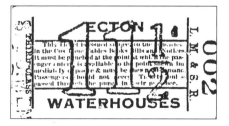

New Circular Tour to Hulme End,

STAFFORDSHIRE.

For the Manifold Valley Railway.

DAY EXCURSION Including Return Journey on the Railway. 6s.

Every SATURDAY, a well-appointed four-in-hand Char-a-banc will leave the Crescent, Buxton, at 9 45 a.m. for 10 a.m. prompt, arriving at Hulme End about 12 15 in time for the train on the Manifold Valley Railway, leaving there at 1 p.m.

The outward journey will be made along the London Road (where extensive views of Buxton and surrounding district are to be seen), and after passing Hindlow, fine views are obtained of the earlier reaches of the Dove Valley and the Peaks, Crombe, Parkers Hill and High Whieldon. A short stay is made at the picturesque villages of Earl Sterndall and Lougnor, Staffordshire being entered shortly before the latter place is reached. The run from Lougnor to Hulme End is rich in sylvan scenery with a charming panorama of Staffordshire Hills.

The Light Railway 2-ft. 6-in. gauge runs from Hulme End down the picturesquely winding Valleys of the Manifold and Hamps to Waterhouses, a distance of about eight miles. These Valleys have been designated the Switzerland of Staffordshire. The "Tramway and Railway World" of 14th July, 1904, says :—" The line passes through some of the most beautiful scenery in the world." The line winds in and out, following the course of the rivers, and each turn brings a varied scene. Items of interest along the route are the now disused Ecton Lead and Copper Mines, Darfar Crags close to Wetton Mill, Thor's Cave, Beeston Tor at the junction of the Manifold and Hamps, the disappearance of the Rivers during the summer into their sub terranean passages to rise again at Ilam, where they join the Dove. The route of the Toy Railway abounds in scenes to interest and please.

Passengers holding **Return Tickets** may alight from and rejoin the Trains at any of the Stations.

Return Trains leave Waterhouses on Saturdays at 2 p.m. and 2 50 p.m.

The Char-a-banc will leave the Light Railway Hotel, Hulme End, at 4 o'clock, and return via Hartington—a model village with and ancient and interesting Church, situate in the midst of the Charles Cotton and Isaac Walton country, and close to the beautiful Beresford Dale.

The Tour comprises in one day, items of Scenic Beauty, Historical interest and associations which are not surpassed in England.

For Descriptive Guide to the Manifold Railway, obtain

" PICTURESQUE STAFFORDSHIRE," Price 6d.

to be obtained at the North Staffordshire Railway Stations, and Booksellers in Buxton.

BOOK EARLY.

W. Webster, Char-a-banc Proprietor, 2, Heath St., Buxton.

Telephone 9Y.

Harry Lockett, Printer, Hanley.

Mrs Dainton

Eric Leslie

Mrs Dainton lived in one of the clusters of cottages at Hulme End. Every year, when the valley once again echoed to the sights and sounds of a steam train, Kit Dainton would be our first customer.

As a schoolteacher she would take pupils on walks down the valley, introducing then to the many wild flowers which grew in abundance. Now, in retirement, she took equal delight in recalling her experiences and happy memories of the railway.

Her late husband was one-time manager at Gilbert's, the Ecton creamery which generated so much traffic for the 'Manifold'.

A favourite story was of how, as children, they would be entertained by a local farmer who had a gold pocket watch which chimed. He would hold out the watch as the children listened, enchanted, as the hour was announced.

When the old farmer died, he was buried in a small plot of his land ringed by trees, just up the road from Hulme End. Such was the magic of this chiming watch, the children would visit the grave and lay with their ears to the ground.

The story had got around that the old boy had been laid to rest in his best suit with the watch still in his waistcoat pocket; by laying down they were sure they could hear it chiming!

.... 60 Churns of milk to go.....

Letter to Tom Dainton, United Dairies, Ecton

From Eric Leslie's Collection

United Dairies (Wholesale) Ltd,
Uttoxeter,
Staffs.
30th October, 1923

Mr T. Dainton,
United Dairies Wholesale Ltd,
Ecton.

Dear Tom

Will you please see the station master at Hulme End first thing on Wednesday morning and tell him that there will be 60 churns of milk to go from Hulme End to Welford's Premier Dairies, Finsbury Park, or Hornsey, I do not quite know which station yet, but it will be one of the two, commencing November 1st.

One load will arrive about 10 o'clock, or 10.30 am and he will want help to unload it and put it somewhere in the shade. The driver will then go back again to Glutton Bridge and bring their milk in, which will get to Hulme End about one or two o'clock.

You had better arrange to stop there another day or two, after Miss Thomas comes back, so as to get these two factories into working order. It will be as well to go over and see them, and see the milk is all right when it comes in at each place, and all properly made up and labelled and everything in order, and see as to what time it may be worked.

You will also want to find some lodgings for the driver Stevenson, as I propose transferring the lorry from Waterhouses to Ecton altogether, as it will be as much as one lorry will do in the daylight in the winter, in that country.

I think we could manage to put it somewhere at Ecton, and the petrol and oil could be stored in the same way as it is at Waterhouses.

Please make all these arrangements and let me know that you have got it all in order when I arrive about 2 o'clock on Wednesday.

Yours faithfully

(Signed) John Dainton

The crew and passengers descended.....
Helped themselves placidly to a healthy pocketful of
good mushrooms.

The Derbyshire Dales

Norman Price

If you enter the Manifold Valley by way of the obscure Hamps Valley from Waterhouses - that tiny village on the road from Leek to Ashbourne, you will be touching upon the tragic march of Bonnie Prince Charlie in 1745.

There used to be a wonderful, almost legendary, light railway that ran between Waterhouses via the Manifold Valley to Hulme End, a total track distance of eight miles.

Realising that they were laying their sacrilegious railway lines through one of the two peerless vales of England, the Directors of the Manifold Valley Light Railway delicately chose a miniature two-foot gauge for serving the scattered hillside farms.

There was no enthusiasm for indecent hurry, nor strict attention to such trivialities as timetables and schedules. When the train chanced to trundle past a luscious wide-scattered patch of mushrooms that had sprung up from the previous day, the engine promptly stopped. The crew and passengers descended and returned to the train in their own good time, having helped themselves placidly to a healthy pocketful of good mushrooms.

The Manifold Valley does have that effect on humans and railway engines. There is a feeling of tranquillity as if a noise has been turned off suddenly, after buzzing for so long that one had ceased consciously to hear it.

[Published by F. Warne & Co. 1953.]

Compiler's comment
Narrow gauge railways in this country seem to bring out a desire amongst passengers to jump down and pick primroses/mushrooms or whatever was to hand. The leisurely rate of progress and close proximity to the beautiful countryside must have had something to do with this.

The Ashover, as usual, reversed this process once by tipping its conductor into the River Amber as he swung from carriage to carriage collecting fares!

Wax seal from
Waterhouses.

"I was well looked after in my four years at Cowlow Farm"--
"Mrs. Bassett was a good cook"

Manifold Memories

Frank Beardmore MBE with David Morgan

Frank joins the LMS at Stoke-on-Trent

The year 1923 was a significant one in railway history. Our local railway, the 'Knotty' (North Staffs. Railway Co.) was grouped into the new London, Midland & Scottish Railway Company.

Later that year, I joined the railway as a cleaner at Stoke-on-Trent shed, the nearest big depôt to my home at Newcastle-under-Lyme. Since leaving school at the age of 13, I'd had two other jobs, working as an office errand boy at Hem Heath Colliery and then with a wagon repair company at Apedale.

In 1923, the family feeling of the 'Knotty' was still very much alive. Most of the locomotives carried the deepish red madder livery of the North Staffordshire. Gradually, though, a more austere black LMS, livery was introduced.

My first duties were in fact cleaning these engines using mineral oil and cotton waste. It was hard work if the engine was dirty. Then the foreman would often put his hand at the back of the wheel spokes to check how thorough we were!

We cleaners meanwhile were learning how the engines worked and had to study the Rule Book. Pay was seven shillings a day at age 20. Sometimes we were called upon to unload locomotive coal by shovel from wagons to a stack on the ground, under the supervision of Nick Carter, the chief stacker. It was tough work: two of us cleaners could unload one wagon a day, comprising 8 to 10 tons.

After a few months, we were examined and I became a passed cleaner. When needed, I could now work as a fireman. On these occasions I was paid 9s. 6d. a day. All our firing turns were recorded towards promotion and when I had completed 313 turns, my regular pay went up to 9s. 6d.

Another duty at Stoke was shovelling coal out of wagons into tubs, which we pushed a few yards before they were lifted by an electric crane to fill locomotive bunkers. Night shift (10 pm to 4 am) was not unpopular, for we were paid time and a quarter. Overtime at night was paid even better - at time and a half!

Forty-six engines had to be coaled up, cleaned and also ashes removed from the ash pit. At 2 am precisely - as indicated by the shed's electric clock - we dropped tools for our 20 minute meal break.

After five years at Stoke depôt, however, a different sort of break in my railway career occurred. As a result of the continuing rationalisation of the LMS Railway, following the Grouping, my work at Stoke was made redundant!

The Move to Hulme End

The process of rationalisation included the closure of some loco sheds. As people's jobs were made redundant, they were transferred to other sheds, as opposed to being sacked. Many shed staff were downgraded; drivers to

Sometimes, my sister came to stay for the weekend.

firemen, and firemen to cleaners. When redundancy hit us at Stoke in 1928, I was offered a job as cleaner in a country area, a remote desolate corner of our county of Staffordshire, at Hulme End. The cleaner there, Bob Powner, was transferred to Gloucester.

So, at age 23, I had to leave the security of home for lodgings at a farm some 25 miles away at Hulme End. On Saturday 8th December, 1928, I took the train from Stoke to Leek, then the Waterhouses branch train, followed by the nine mile 2 ft 6 in. gauge Manifold Valley train up to Hulme End. Here I took over Bob Powner's old lodgings at Cowlow Farm, close to the station.

The farm was owned by Walter Bassett and family, whose father, John, a noted local landowner, had been one of the promoters of the Manifold Valley Light Railway. I was well looked after in my four years at Cowlow Farm; in fact, we lived off the fat of the land. Sometimes my sister came to stay for a weekend and she was even provided with a fire in her bedroom!

Work at Hulme End started next morning, Sunday, for the Manifold Valley Line had a service of mixed trains seven days a week, particularly to convey milk wagons from the creamery at Ecton.

I will recall my duties as a passed cleaner during a typical spring day. I started work at six o'clock in the morning by unlocking the shed and then lit the electric light run off the coach batteries. The line had two 2-6-4 tank locomotives built by Kitson of Leeds in 1904. They were named *E.R. Calthrop* and *J.B. Earle*. The fire of one was lit with wood, cotton-waste and coal, and when it was built up sufficiently, I cleaned the black-liveried engine with cotton-waste and mineral oil. The following day, I would dry-wipe it to clean it. Cleaning the coaches, though, was not my responsibility.

Later, I would slip back over the field to the farm for breakfast, comprising porridge, bacon and eggs and Staffordshire oat cakes, with tea to drink. Mrs Bassett was a good cook!

The farm was lit by paraffin lamps, for it had no electricity in those days. We at the shed were lucky to tap electricity from the coach batteries! Back at the shed, the steam pressure was gradually increasing as the fire was built up and spread out, and more coal put on. One day, when I was off duty, my work was covered by Fred Burrows, who had cycled the 25 miles from Stoke on his Hercules bike. He failed to put enough coal on the fire and the steam pressure was low. So, the engine crew had to lever the engine to the coal stage using pinch bars. But they made it, though, for the 9 o'clock train!

Preparing for Departure at Hulme End

When steam pressure was sufficient, I took the engine to the coaling plant by the water tower and shovelled coal into the bunker. Then the tanks were filled up from the water tower. Water was pumped up into the tank from the stream using a water wheel in the nearby field. That is why Frank Salt, the driver, was

"The ashes were shovelled into a wagon for disposal"

LESLIE.

so keen on saving steam. If the engine blew off, that water, pumped up from the field, was being wasted!

Frank, the driver, and Dennis Reynolds, his fireman, came on duty at about 8 o'clock and they now took charge. Dennis would keep an eye on the fire and polish up the brasses with Brasso provided by the company. Everything had to be spick and span. Frank and Dennis then assembled the train in the platform.

Once the crew had taken over, I could turn my attention to maintenance on the second engine, which had been in use the previous week. From the smokebox the plugs had to be taken out and the tubes cleaned with rods to get rid of the soot. The ashes were shovelled into a wagon for disposal. The boiler had to be washed out. Being a limestone area, there was lime in the local water which led to a build-up of scale in the boiler tubes. This had to be removed. I have my suspicions that my predecessor, Bob Powner, did not do this very thoroughly! Other duties included checking the shed and keeping it tidy. I could take my time over the work and do it well, taking the occasional tea-break. My shift was 6 am to 2 pm, with no overtime in winter months.

After Frank Salt retired, Dennis Reynolds took over as driver, with a new fireman. On a Saturday, after my shift, I usually went home to Stoke to visit my family. Dennis, who was a very considerate person, suggested I go home earlier by starting work at 4 am and finish at noon. We asked the Superintendent, Mr Lonsdale, at Stoke for permission, and he suggested I start work at 4 am each morning, which would allow more time for the engine to raise steam. Mark you, most days, apart from Saturday and when the fitters came from Stoke, I kept to the 6 am to 2 pm hours.

Because of the daily service, we each worked a seven day week for two out of three weeks. To allow Dennis and Frank each a Sunday off, I did firing turns two out of three Sundays. For this, I was paid time and a half, and the turns were credited towards seniority.

I was very settled at Hulme End. However, after four years in this remote corner of Staffordshire, the company was doing more shut-downs in the area and the future of the Manifold Valley line itself was not very secure. So, in 1932, I found myself transferred even further afield, to Redditch Shed in Worcestershire. I remained there in railway service until retirement in the mid-1960s. Not long after leaving Hulme End, I was joined at Redditch by driver Dennis Reynolds, my lifelong friend, who lived to reach the mature age of 91.

Compiler's footnote

A few months after providing this series of memories, Frank was taken into Bromsgrove Hospital where he died on 6th August, 1990, aged 86, and ending the final link with the Leek & Manifold Valley Light Railway.

Valley of Dreams

D.M. Smith

On March 1st last the LMSR issued the following public notice from the district offices at Stoke-on-Trent.

Notice is hereby given that the Manifold Valley Light Railway section of the Company's line, Waterhouses to Hulme End, will be closed for the conveyance of all classes of traffic on and from Monday, March 12th, 1934.

Lying in the north-east corner of Staffordshire, the railway, opened in June 1904, was connected with the Manchester-Uttoxeter branch at Leek by a standard gauge line from Waterhouses. As no trains ran on Sundays on this 2 ft 6 in. gauge line, which was the subject of an illustrated article by Mr Charles F. Clapper in the *Railway Magazine* of October 1932, the last day of actual service was Saturday, 10th March.

To go over the line, therefore, on the closing day, after travelling by night from Euston, I approached Leek by an early morning train from Manchester. When reached, both Leek and Waterhouses were beneath a three-inch blanket of snow, and this promised for those who were to make the journey the good fortune of seeing the Manifold Valley, one of the most lovely in England, in the most beautiful conditions.

After much shunting, the little train, composed of one passenger car and two or three goods vehicles, left Waterhouses almost half an hour late with only seven passengers. We were not even promised that the train would never be late again!

Soon we had puffed and rattled through the valley of the Hamps and entered that of the Manifold. Here in the stillness and silence the snow lay thick, while the tops of the valley sides, 400 ft high, were clothed in a soft, white, mist.

Only one stop was made during the eight-mile journey, a passenger alighting at Grindon Halt. The atmosphere of the valley was amazing, and the gaunt pinnacle of Thor's Cave, sinister in its predominance on any other day, rose mysteriously fairy-like into the softening mist.

At Hulme End, the terminus, reality returned, for it seemed as if we had passed through a valley of dreams. There was considerable activity here, a place which consists of several cottages and a Light Railway Hotel, now, alas, an anachronism, as after all, even on a light railway the last day of service must have a certain importance.

Station equipment had to be collected and returned: incidentally, many of the tickets that were being issued were of the pre-Grouping North Staffordshire Railway era. The rolling stock and buildings, on the other hand, were so far as the staff was concerned, to be abandoned as they stood, and instructions had been received that the two locomotives, one of which returned from an overhauling at Crewe only three weeks before, should be greased and left in the sheds.

The staff was being transferred to other parts of the LMS system, and a wry smile from a cleaner was the only answer to the suggestion that this might mean rather more work than that entailed in the running of two trains a day.

[Published in the *Railway Magazine*, May 1934.]

Flood at Sparrowlee

Eric Leslie

Just before the line closed, there was a heavy downpour which resulted in part of the track being in danger of being washed away. A substantial stretch was flooded around Sparrowlee and a train was marooned until the guard took off his shoes and socks, rolled up his trousers and paddled to the nearest phone point.

These were plugs where a portable hand-set could be plugged in enabling the guard to keep in contact. Telegraph poles along the route carried these phone plugs at set intervals.

The guard also had a tramway type ticket machine to enable him to book fares along the unmanned halts in the valley.

Flood at Sparrowlee

We set Mr Wood down at Beeston, and he stands
to wave his last to the train.

Last Train Forever: Valley of Locked Stations

From our Special Correspondent

Leek, Sunday

Last night, one of the most picturesque and romantic railways in Great Britain went into retirement, and today, seven little stations lining a lonely, tortuous track through the lovely Manifold Valley near here are locked up.

Ever since June 1904 the Manifold Valley Light Railway has carried farmers and their produce to and from market, and borne holiday makers along the side of the famous 'disappearing river' at a bustling 15 mph. Road competition, mainly, has brought it to an end.

A staff of seven were employed upon it: tomorrow they will be finding their way to new homes and fresh tasks at LMS centres. The two locomotives and the rolling stock lie in their sheds at one or other end of the 8½ miles of track.

The Only One

'There is no other one in Great Britain of this gauge', the driver told me, as we waited for the last journey of all, from Waterhouses (where the broad-gauge railway meets the little one) to Hulme End, the lonely terminal four miles from Hartington, in Derbyshire. From the distant station they brought up on the previous trip the chairs and tables, weighing machines, clock, tickets etc. The fireman brought his wife and two children to catch the broad gauge train for Leek and a new home. The last sightseers came up with it.

We are taking back just a handful of regular passengers for their last homeward journey. Mr Arthur John Salt, the guard, is conducting the train for the last time in 20 years. Mr William Wood, aged 78, owner of Beeston Tor Farm, travelled on the first train 30 years ago. He has journeyed regularly on market days by it since. Now, very regretfully, he is seeing the last of it.

The Last Post

The big train on the broad gauge line blows a sort of whistled Last Post. The little train whistles wanly in reply.

Mist thick and white fills the valley. Over the rugged walls and the rounded slopes alike a chequered sheet of snow lies thickly, like 'dust sheets' thrown over a mansion's treasures when the household departs.

'I remember your father' says Mr Wood to the guard. Mr Salt senior, it seems, drove the first train and went on driving it day after day until four years ago.

'For 16 years my father and I took the train backwards and forwards together', the guard replies.

'I remember the first day', says Mr Wood.

'The engine and coaches were all new and bright. About 200 people went on the first trip. Seats and awnings were fitted on the long, iron trucks that were meant to carry long loads like tree-trunks. Passengers travelled in the goods vans, too.'

Underground River

The guard talks of the beauties of the route and the things holiday passengers want to know about.

'Look at that river' he says. 'Its dry like that for miles except after very heavy rainfall. It goes underground at Wetton Mill and comes up again at Ilam, some miles away.'

We set Mr Wood down at Beeston Tor, and he stands to wave his last at the train.

The guard points out the milk factory at Ecton. He says, 'We used to bring 300 cans of milk a day to it; now it is closed and the work divided among depôts in many parts of the country. We used to carry more passengers and a lot of corn, but most of that goes by road now.'

The Fire Raked Out

All along the line he has been locking up the waiting rooms and offices for the last time. Now we are at Hulme End. The driver and fireman rake out the glowing fire of the locomotive and run it into the shed. The guard locks up the last gate. Tomorrow he walks four miles to Hartington for a train to his next job at Uttoxeter!

Brass plate fixed to Hulme End Station building.

Leek & Manifold Valley Light Railway

Statement Leaflet, 23rd July, 1937

The History of the Means of Access to the Valley

The Leek & Manifold Valley Light Railway Company was formed by local residents, landowners, farmers and business people for the development of the district in North Staffordshire near the Manifold Valley. The district is chiefly rich agricultural land, and suitable means of transport were considered necessary owing to the difficult roads which pass over steep hills of more than 1,000 sq. ft above sea level.

The necessity was realised by the Government who gave Free Grants of £17,500 and a loan of £7,500. Assistance was given by the Staffordshire County Council who granted loans of £15,000. The people of the district, in addition to providing over £16,000 in Share Capital, undertook to guarantee the interest payments on County Council loans and in consequence paid special rates for this purpose for many years.

It was necessary to obtain further capital and in 1912 the North Staffordshire Railway Company provided £8,000 in Debenture Stock, but unfortunately for local interests they imposed restrictive conditions which were then calculated to prevent the profitable working of the railway and time has shown that these calculations were well founded.

The working of the light railway became controlled by the NSR and eventually the LMS and both companies by neglecting the opportunities of obtaining traffic, brought about a position which compelled the abandonment of the railway.

Immediately on the closing of the light railway, local authorities saw an opportunity of obtaining greater advantages from the abandoned railway track than they had been receiving from the limited working of the light railway.

The Staffordshire County Council were petitioned to take over the track for the purpose of converting it to a roadway. After refusing this request, on hearing representations from other interests, the County Council agreed to take over the track for its conversion to a *footpath only*. This had the effect of saving the track and preventing the demolition of the bridges. Had the bridges been demolished, the track would have been useless for any purpose.

The Position Today (1937)

An Area Committee representing the district served by the Manifold Valley Light Railway was formed at the instance of the Cheadle Rural District Council. The views of the committee are given below:

The need for suitable means of transport is just as urgent today as it was before the construction of the light railway. Travelling over the steep and high hills is a wastage from a business point of view, and causes hardship to those who reside and earn their living in the district.

A MOTOR ROAD on the track of the railway would provide easy access from the district to the main roads and 'bus routes which exist at Hulme End and Waterhouses. Travellers from the south would find the road a gateway to the villages bordering on the valley, and to good roads leading to Buxton, Bakewell, Matlock and other parts of north-west Derbyshire and beyond. Such travellers would include business people, local government officials, doctors, and veterinary surgeons, and those travelling for pleasure.

Now that the light railway has been ABANDONED by the LMS Company, it is claimed that the local people who established the railway by their labours and sacrifices have a moral right to first consideration in the disposal of the residue of their own creation. £50,000 was expended on providing this railway track for the definite purpose of carrying passengers and goods for the benefit of the district. The value still remains if the track is used for its proper purpose as a roadway.

The Salient Points

The proposed use of the railway track as a 'footpath' only is unsatisfactory. The Ramblers' Association states 'It is the ambition of ramblers to dodge hard roads. One gets so much of them in the city that it is a relief to feel something soft underneath one's feet'. The Ramblers' Association also protest against 'footing it on a hard unsympathetic road'.

There are ramblers on this Area Committee who have the same feelings. For the benefit of the real rambler it may be pointed out that there are HUNDREDS OF MILES OF PUBLIC FOOTPATHS in existence already which give fine access to the valley. These are the paths recommended to the real rambler. From them he will get the most enjoyment - wonderful scenery, a bracing atmosphere and endless variety.

Something has been heard about the iniquity of motorists and the effect of allowing motors in the valley. There are undesirable elements in all sections and classes.

Farmers have every reason to complain of the depredations of irresponsible ramblers, and are entitled to demand a road to give supervision. This does not mean that the rambler can, or should be, denied access.

But what justification is there for excluding motorists as a body? There are many lovers of the countryside who are not young and strong, yet get health and pleasure by viewing the beauty spots of the country. The fact that they are unable to walk long distances cannot justify their exclusion.

As to the conduct of motorists, those who offend may be educated along with the worst class of 'hiker'.

The Area Committee contend that this 'pseudo-footpath' is of no benefit to the county ratepayers, county and other local government officials, doctors, and veterinary surgeons, the real ramblers, the lover of the countryside, or any section.

The committee are satisfied that the above mentioned people would derive considerable advantage from a motor road, and that such a road is essential to the well-being of the residents in the area and the important business of agriculture. Above all, they are taking this stand in the interests of all road users and the community at large as a matter of equity and justice.

[By the Chairman and Members of the AREA COMMITTEE representing the parishes served by the light railway.]

LEEK & MANIFOLD VALLEY LIGHT RAILWAY.

A view of Thor's Cave taken from above the old Railway Track.

STATEMENT

by the Chairman and Members of the AREA COMMITTEE representing the Parishes served by the LIGHT RAILWAY.

23rd July, 1937.

Bank Holiday Special !

Extracts from a Diary, 1936

G.V. Wingfield-Digby

Extracts from entries concerning the Manifold Valley and its narrow gauge railway, from the 34th volume of my Journal, September 1936, some 18 months after the closure of the line, but before the track had been taken up and when it was still as it had been when abandoned in March 1934.

Wednesday 9th September, 1936 . We now journeyed on to Waterhouses, where the standard gauge line from Leek ends, and the narrow gauge Manifold Valley railway begins - both now abandoned. Proceeding along a steep lane , we crossed a very deep ford, and meandering along a winding, twisting way, consisting of thick mud with large stones thrown about and embedded in it.

At last we considered it desirable to descend to the valley, which we achieved by an extremely steep grass-grown slope in many places practically at a gradient of one-in-one. The hills on either side of the valley (which was so narrow as to allow no more than the small-gauge line of the single track) rose on either side, almost sheer for some 1,200 ft in places much enriched by hanging wood.

The delightful narrow gauge railway (closed in 1934) twisted and turned amid splashing and gurgling waters, often invisible and sometimes tumbling into silvery cataracts. This wayward stream was crossed and re-crossed by the little railway - altogether some 36-40 times by hollow floorless bridges of varying heights and lengths.

The sleepers here were replaced by large heavy cross-beams widely spaced, with a frowning abyss between each. The bridge could be crossed by slender iron sheetways on either side but these were very rusted and uncertain in their support.

There were also some 10 or 11 little halts with small derelict shelters but no platforms. A remarkable point about these was their very complete isolation, far from habitation of any kind, and accessible only by field gates (and, except, for Grindon and Ecton) without any paths.

The spot where we struck the twisting line was beyond Sparrowlee Halt. Presently R. turned back in order to take his motor car round by the rough track to Grindon Halt, which proved to be an extremely difficult proceeding. Meanwhile, I went on, past Beeston Tor Halt, with the mighty tor towering straight above it and the river twisting and winding more than ever.

Here, there was a vehicle of ancient passenger stock, now converted into a shelter, and somewhat ruinous. One of many surviving notices on the line bore evidence of the original owners 'The North Staffordshire Railway'.

The shelter at Grindon Halt had its windows so completely smashed that the fragments of glass were sprinkled over the entire floor like hoar-frost.

A steep, winding ascent, rough and stony, brought me face to face with a large ferocious-looking bull, with lowered horns and snorting nostrils. I deemed it expedient to put a five-bar gate between myself and this monster, and here stayed for upwards of an hour in a wild field, bordered by miles of broken stone, half-ruinous. I spent the time watching the movements of my bull and some cows and poultry: in seeking to keep as dry as possible from the light but steady drizzle, and in throwing stones into a deep and dark pond that was possibly the top of a long-abandoned mine-shaft.

When R. at last arrived, we partook of such refreshment as we had with us (remains from yesterday) and walked along further up the valley, which still twisted and turned amidst colossal heights, overhung by glorious woods.

Crossing the river by a narrow timber bridge off the railway a long, steep and very slippery climb brought us to the grand mouth of Thor's Cave, a prominent and frowning gulf, high up the hillside and visible many miles, at least, it would be visible many miles down the valley had it not been for the latter's incessant twistings and turnings.

This, by far the finest cave in Staffordshire, well repaid the arduous climb, sticky and slippery as it was . [Here follows an exhaustive description of the ramifications of the interior passages and recesses of the cave.]

The cold air from the cave had now cooled us, and we descended the steep and slippery slope, crossed the river, and were soon again upon the little rusted and abandoned railway. We now continued our journey along the valley, passed more halts with their dilapidated shelters and through stretches of the line that had now become very overgrown and in many ways, the more pretty, as nature once more triumphed over Man.

Before the halt at Butterton (miles from the village it served) there was a tunnel, the only bore on the line. What a dismal place, with the water trickling and streaming down the walls, with a tiny arc of daylight peeping in at either end. It started to become darker as on advanced further into it, and our voices echoed eerily from the slimy walls. It is sad to think that it is now two years since the last little train thundered through it, and that never more will it be of further use but only even ourselves saw the day that it will tumble in and decay to its extinction. Just beyond was another hollow bridge, extremely rusty, with the river gurgling and chattering far below.

A mile or so further we reached the Ecton Halt, with extensive copper mines on the side of the hill, all long abandoned, and the ruined relics reminding us of ruined fortunes. We examined some of these and discovered an underground lake and deep, dark water issuing from the outlet of an in-filled shaft.

Here, too, there was a dilapidated milk factory, the abandonment of which, some years ago, spelt the final ruin of the railway. It was indeed a forlorn, desolate place that reminded me of Foxdale in the Isle of Man, with its long forsaken lead mines.

The final (and very long) mile was less interesting. The valley petered out into rough pastures and, after several more of the hollow iron bridges, the railway came to an end at Hulme End, amid scenes of abandonment.

At a cottage at Hulme End we refreshed ourselves with drinks before starting back to collect our gear, which had been left at Grindon Halt. R., However, decided to get a lift on a motor-cycle to a spot not far off, reached by tortuous roads, byways and tracks.

But they lost their way, and R. lost his, so completely on the return journey that he ran into an entirely unclimbable hill in the dark. His motor ran backwards, and he had to jump out to save his life. But he had the presence of mind, however, to put some stones from a wall to stop the vehicle, and, with the combined efforts of five or six sturdy villagers pushing with all their might, succeeded in reaching the top in safety. Meanwhile, I walked alone along the line in the dusk.

How gloomy the tunnel looked, down in the gathering darkness. How threatening, how stern, how frowning! I then crossed the high iron bridge over the rushing river and make my way to the road. Here I stayed for about an hour and a quarter, in the increasing blackness of night, and overhung by dense and clustered woods. I wrote notes for this journal by the light of my lamp and smoked several cigarettes as I waited.

What a very dark night it was! The blackness settled down so completely that even the sky was entirely invisible. One might have been in the deepest recesses of a cavern or in the very grave itself.

Shortly after nine o'clock I decided to find my own way back, by the road. Even by the light of my lantern, it was not easy to follow the way. Very often there was something of a precipice on one side or both: and then there was the peril of the abandoned shafts of the forsaken Ecton mines.

Once, I did run off my route, and, on another occasion, was completely perplexed by the intricacies of the way.

But, all the while, there was the gurgling song of unseen waters tumbling and splashing in the river down in the valley: or pouring down the hillside in invisible cataracts: or, quite often, thundering and splashing down the limestone. All the way, indeed, these waters never ceased to sing, cheering my passage in the darkness, adding to the glamour of the night.

At last I reached the CTC cottage at Hulme End and, after a long wait, R. arrived to tell me his strange experiences, and we wearily retired to rest.

Thursday 10th September, 1936. Drizzle nearly all day, cool. Before departing from Hulme End I wrote a little of this journal. [The rest of this day is not concerned with the Manifold Valley.] We arrived back at Hulme End at last, at about 12.45 and had to knock the people up. We retired at 3 am.

Friday 11th September, 1936. Chiefly overcast, moderate temperature. During the forenoon I examined the deserted station at Hulme End, the little terminus of the narrow gauge railway that 'Ran from nowhere to nowhere', as it was aptly described.

It was a depressing sight, overgrown, rusty and forlorn. The nameboard lay on its face across the track in melancholy fashion, and, when I tried to raise it, I found it rotting away. Beside the usual offices and waiting rooms (locked, but looking dismal enough through the broken windows) there are various sheds for repairs and rolling stock (all empty, but in good condition) a decayed coal tip, and seven overgrown sidings. It was indeed the 'dead-end' of a very sorry wreck of a most attractive railway.

. . . Despite its undisputed glory, we are not sorry to leave it (i.e. Dovedale), and to journey over very steep and lonely moorland roads for a further, and final, inspection of our adorable and solitary Manifold Valley.

We started this time from the Waterhouses end. I wanted to complete my survey by covering the ground between there and beyond Sparrowlee Halt, where our previous inspection had started. There were the usual towering heights and gorgeous hanging woods, the same hollow iron bridges over rock-strewn torrents, twelve in number in the four miles or so of our journey in the Manifold today.

Turning a corner suddenly, we were surprised (and a little shocked), to encounter a young fellow cuddling a girl. `The fellow jumped up at once and turned away; his mistress was still fastening up her dress as we passed. I did not suspect what was afoot until we were quite abreast. The terrible scowl that the girl gave me I shall surely never forget.

Night had descended when we started back. The valley was wrapt alike in blackness and in silence. The hidden waters and the screeching of little owls in the depths of the wooded slopes, which stood out in palls beneath the darkening sky. Seldom before had I discovered so grand and a valley, of solitude and silence - unspoiled, unsullied and unknown.

The return journey was somewhat hazardous, it was black as a cavern, and a false step between the sleepers on one of the hollow bridges would have meant a plunge into the abyss beneath, with, at the least, a broken leg. Moreover, the gate was open into a field of bulls which could stray upon the line . . . and we went into them.

Progress was slow, as, one after the other, we encountered the hazardous bridges and crept across the rusty, narrow metal-way beside them, that swayed beneath our weight.

Frequently, we would halt, to give our wearied eyes at rest, or to enjoy the silence and the utter blackness of the night.

But, at last, the eleventh bridge was safely conquered, the danger of the bulls left far behind, and we emerged on to the by-road at the level crossing (that was) at Waterhouses. And so the great looming of the wooded hills, the murmur and the song of the rushing waters, and the many twisted valleys were left behind.

We found welcome at a small cottage, where we knocked up the occupant to provide us with a simple supper - the first refreshment (at 11 pm) that we had received since breakfast.

Saturday 12th September, 1936. Rain all day, moderate temperature to cool, with much mist. Before leaving Waterhouses, I examined the few remains of the rolling stock of the Manifold Railway.

These included a few very rusted trucks (dated 1904), an engine protected by a tarpaulin, apparently in fair condition, but of a type long obsolete, and a brake van (also dated 1904) in an advanced state of decay. How new, and fresh and strong and bright, 30 years ago!, thought I. And now, so tumbling to pieces that it could scarcely hold itself together in order to be trundled away to the breaker's yard!

Steam in the Manifold

Eric Leslie

Every year the spectacle of a steam engine and train running over part of the old track-bed could be enjoyed for three consecutive weekends.

This time though, the gauge was 10¼ in., but it still didn't detract from the sights and sounds which had been absent from the valley for so long.

Hard-working volunteers from Belle Engineering at nearby Sheen, gave up their time to lay almost a mile of temporary, prefabricated track, run the train and then dismantle the whole thing afterwards. All the materials had to be manhandled into position, after doing a days' work often until late into the night just to ensure everything was ready on time.

The Highway Dept then owners of the station site, allowed the use of the old building, which housed an exhibition of photographs and memorabilia of the old line. A minibus was organised by the Peak Park people to take passengers along the old trackbed to extend further the ride down the valley and through Swainsley tunnel and beyond. Once there was a horse-drawn carriage for rides around Hulme End. All proceeds went to the Macmillan Fund for cancer relief.

'Steam in the Manifold' was extremely successful and 'regulars' came along every year. So much interest led to the formation of the Manifold Valley Railway Society. The aim was to try and ensure that the old station building would be preserved as the only artefact, along with the engine shed, which had survived more or less intact, from the old line.

The old building, which still contained its typical ticket hatch window, was in dire near of first aid. The engine shed opposite had recently been re-roofed and was used as a garage for the council's road vehicles and was not, therefore under the same threat.

Not so the booking office - with its tree growing out of the chimney pot, missing canopy, sagging roof and walls and general air of impending doom. Even the rain had found alternative ways of reaching the ground from the rusting roof sheets.

Fortunately, an emergency package of repairs was put in hand by the council and the old building stood up to the weather much better, enabling a more extensive restoration to take place recently.

Without the intervention of the 'Manifold Mob' and the good relationship with the Highways Dept it would have undoubtedly been lost for ever.

Perhaps one day it would be possible to have a permanent railway presence at Hulme End. I sincerely hope so. Something which serves to remind the public that here once ran a beautiful railway, in the forefront of the best technical practice when it was built, and even today, ahead of its time with the practical use of transporter wagons. And good to look at!

SYX

LESLIE.

Steam again in the "Manifold Valley"